The Road to SUCCESS

Winner Torborg

Bread of Life International Ministries

II

"The Road to Success" by Winner Torborg
Copyright © 2011 by Winner Torborg of Bread of Life
International Ministries. All rights reserved. (www.bolim.org)
ISBN - 10:0982693109 **ISBN - 13:**9780982693100

Credentials

Almost all his life people around Winner have been trying to get the best of him. Winner was always the kind of guy who, if he found a good cause, would do he best to help. He was never one for falsity although he did have a hard time catching others in their lies.

In September of 1980, Winner Torborg made the life changing confession that Jesus is Lord; he was age of 19 years at the time. Four years later, September of 1984, at a Christian meeting Winner asked for and received the anointing of the Holy Spirit; right then everything he had read in the Bible came alive to him and his ability to learn and grasp knowledge of God's Word increased mightily. The next day he answered the call of God to step into the ministry, mainly as a teacher.

As a teacher, Winner had to learn and retain knowledge from the Bible and from watching how other people act in their lives. In September of 1985, Winner began a newsletter ministry called Bread of Life. He started by writing to a group of church people, and his ministry grew. In 1997, Winner put his ministry on the World Wide Web, and the name changed to Bread of Life International Ministries. He is now reaching people from all around the world in many different languages.

Winner also writes for many online magazines and for Bread of Life International Ministries (www.bolim.org).

Why I use many versions of the Bible?

I do this because there is not one version that has every verse right; none of the modern versions have been translated directly from the original Hebrew, Aramaic and Greek. If I only used the King James you would get only a King James approach to God's Word; likewise, if I only used the NIV you would get an NIV approach. I wanted to share the clearest approach that I can so I must use many versions. As an ancient saying that many people claim as their own goes, "There is more than one way to go up a mountain." I use many Bibles but you must let the Holy Spirit guide you. And I suggest that you get many versions also. In one version a verse may be quoted one way and in another the same verse is quoted a totally different way.

VIII

The Road to Success
Table of contents

Special Note From Me to You

I did a study about success because, just like everyone else, I also want success in my life; I want to be a successful person. Some of my findings may well astonish some of you as you read.

Winner

Prologue

Everyone wants to be a success; but many, if not most, of these people have differing definitions of success. They want success, but they neither know what true success is nor how to obtain it; they wouldn't know success if it bit them in the nose.

Some people have said, "To be a successful person you need to hang around with successful people." But that is a catch 22 because if you are not a successful person and you don't know what success is then you wouldn't know who is a successful person whom you could hang out with. It is just like, "To be wise hang out with the wise." That only works if you know what wisdom is.

In this book we are going to look at success from two perspectives, the perspective of the world and the perspective of the Bible.

Chapter 1

Is It Money?

Some people whom I have polled have the idea that success mean having lots of money and letting everyone know it. But what does money have to do with being successful?

There are people who own multi-million dollar businesses, who live in condos in high-rise buildings, people whom others have wanted to be like because they are multi-millionaires. Are these people really successful?

Well, let's look at this type of people. They probably have been working 18 hours a day, 7 days a week for 20, 30, even 40 years to get to that position. Working so hard they neglected having a mate, a social life, or even fun. If they are married their marriage may be suffering; and if they have children their children may not know their father or mother. There is a great problem with this kind of life because everyone will try to take advantage of the one who is in such a position, and someone will, eventually, try to take his or her position.

Oh, he or she may be kind every once in a while and give some money to help someone but that is not what they rely upon to build their status.

Let's look at some examples of people with, as they say, boocoos of money. First let's look at Ebenezer Scrooge. Here was a man who was intent on having money. He worked 16-20 hours per day, 7 days per week. He didn't believe in holidays or having fun, and he didn't believe in helping anyone financially, his past might have had something to do with that. Undoubtedly, you have seen the movie about him, A Christmas Carol.

Ebenezer Scrooge was a very rich man, and one reason was because he worked 16-20 hours each day, he didn't take days off-no weekends and no holidays. You know what he said about Christmas, I'm sure he said that about every holiday. I'm sure you have seen the movie, at least one of the variations of it, more than once. So, you know what he thought of the poor homeless children or beggars on the street, I don't need to quote any of it.

With all the money that he had he could have eaten filet mignon every night. But what did the movie show him having before he went to bed? Porridge, a poor man's meal.

Although he was so very rich he lost the love of his life and much more. It seems to me that the man was as successful as his partner, Marley.

It's a good thing that the visitation from those three spirits turned Scrooge's ways because no one can spend any money after they are dead.

Now let's look at another famous person, this time it's a real man. Howard Hughes was one of the richest men in the world; he had many inventions under his belt. He made a name for himself in the public's eye early on in life, in the film industry, in aeronautics and as a philanthropist.

In his early 20's he became a film producer and made some very high-budget movies. He also began an industrious life in the aviation field and came out with some famous aircraft such as the Spruce Goose.

This man could afford not to work at all in his later years, which was good because he contracted a mental illness and secluded himself for months at a time. He wound up buying hotels, casinos and restaurants; he started a medial institute.

Most people remember Howard Hughes as a man who secluded himself from the public, a paranoid obsessive man, a man whom it was hard to get to. But he was a man of vision who just couldn't continue in the life that he started. In the medical field he is remembered for his philanthropy for the Howard Hughes Medical Institute, in the film industry he is remembered as a maverick, and in the aeronautics industry he is remembered for Hughes Aircraft.

These people had great money, money enough to buy Fort Knox ten times over; but no money in the world can buy anyone's way to heaven. It can't even buy true happiness on earth.

In A Christmas Carol, if it weren't for the three Christmas spirits, do you think Scrooge would have died a happy man? When Howard Hughes died in 1976 do you think he was happy?

I'm sure you can think of some very rich people who are alive today, people with money running out their ears. Look at their lives and answer this simple question. Are they truly happy?

Does Personal Success Depend Upon Your Social Status?

I have met some very popular people in my life. I've met football heroes, basketball legends, baseball superstars; the same goes for hockey and tennis. I've been on television myself and I have met others who were very well known actors and news people. And I'm sure that many of you have also, whether you knew it or not.

Let's look at George Herman Ruth Jr., you may know him better as 'Babe.' Now, here was a man who, when he was a kid, was sent away to school and mentored by the Head of

Discipline at St. Mary's Industrial School for Boy's, a reformatory and orphanage. He had a rough childhood but was taught to be a good tailor.

The man actually started in baseball as a pitcher and then a right fielder but his skills as a hitter soon surfaced. He quickly rose to fame and used his influence to make baseball our national sport. He was famous off the field for his charity but also known as a reckless man.

Then we have Abner Doubleday, the man that is widely known as the inventor of baseball. He was actually a general in the Federal Army during the Civil War. He received some notarization for that, and then the baseball issue was disputed.

Whether Doubleday trumped up the idea that he invented baseball or not it stands that Babe Ruth gave it a boost for sure.

There are many athletes who prioritize their athletic prowess and have order in their lives; and then there are those who don't. The former work hard to build for themselves a standing in the sports world and can get stuck up and prideful, they don't realize that their awesome abilities are not theirs to simply build up their own names.

Some of them glorify God or recognize their mother or the man who trained them; and others don't. In the lifetime of sports, especially in the past decade, there have been players who would make a public show of their faith in God by writing a scripture verses on their helmets or their hands, when they would raise them. Some football players would raise their hands to God in praise when they would make a touchdown.

I talked to a man who worked on a pit crew in NASCAR a few years ago. He told me that many people in the racing circuit are Christians. When Dale Earnhardt hit that embankment and went to his final resting ground many people turned to Jesus.

Chapter 2

Poll

How do you define success?

When I accepted this assignment, to write a book about true success, the first thing I did was poll the average person on the streets, in the stores, and on the Internet and asked them this question.

Some said that to them it is to have friends and family whom they can count on and who can count on them. Others say that success means being able to be a Jesus to the world.

To some success means that you can hear the Father say, "Well done," at the end of your life and "Welcome to heaven," with a great smile. But some think that just because they have confessed Jesus as Lord they have achieved success.

So far, none of these have said anything about being happy, having money, or doing a job, working.

People have said that success means being able to be happy at your job, wherever you work, no matter what the pay. Some said that it was being able to be at peace in all situations and no matter what goes on around you.

One person, who allowed me to quote him but gave me no name, said, "For me success is when one sets themselves towards honorable goals and endlessly strives to meet said goals. You don't have to get everything you desire to be successful. But working hard and pursuing that which is most important to you in itself is success. I see it this way because not everyone can make their biggest dreams come true. But those who never give up and push themselves as people are just as successful as those that reach their goals. The effort of such is the true trademark of a champion."

I like that. While others talked vaguely about doing something this man talks very specifically about setting honorable goals; and not only setting them but also not stopping until those goals are achieved. And, being that the goal is a God-inspired dream, the pursuit of that dream is in itself success if the person is, indeed, going at it full force.

Steve Carney, fellow author and teacher defines success like so, "To me, success means simple obedience to God. In God's kingdom, success doesn't necessarily mean status, power, fame, or wealth." If it depended upon those elements then most of America and the world would have to live without the possibility of success.

Most of the people whom I polled at Victory Christian Center have said that it is achieving goals. One of my respected friends said that success is holding onto your dreams and not letting anyone talk you out of them. He said that it is also achieving them to the best of your ability so that, when this life ends, you can give it to God and hear Him say, "Well done."

My dad sent me this quote from an unknown author, "It is not the critic who counts; not the man/woman who points out how the strong man/woman stumbles, or where the doer of deeds could have done them better. The credit belongs to the man/woman who is actually in the arena, whose face is marred by dust and sweat and blood; who strives valiantly; who errs, and comes short again and again, because there is no effort without error and shortcoming; but who does actually strive to do the deeds; who knows the great enthusiasms, the great devotions; who spends himself (or herself) in a worthy cause; who at the best knows in the end the triumph of high achievement, and who at the worse, if he (or she) fails, at least fails while daring greatly, so that his/her place shall never be with those cold and timid souls who know neither victory nor defeat."

In this verse Jesus was talking about worldly success when He said,

> "When people realize it is the living God you are presenting and not some idol that makes them feel good, they are going to turn on you, even people in your own family. There is a great irony here: proclaiming so much love, experiencing so much hate! But don't quit. Don't cave in. It is all well worth it in the end. It is not [worldly] success you are after in such times but survival. Be survivors! Before you've run out of options, the Son of Man will have arrived," (Matthew 10:21 The Message) ['worldly' added].

However you call it, whatever words you use, success has nothing to do with money or fame. Ability to achieve what Jesus commanded you to do has much more to do with success than material property. But, how do we achieve that status of being successful?

> "And don't for a minute let this Book of The Revelation be out of mind. Ponder and meditate on it day and night, making sure you practice everything written in it. Then you'll get where you're going; then you'll succeed," (Joshua 1:8 The Message).

This verse makes it pretty plain that there is no success without the Word of God in your life. The Book of The Revelation is the book about the love and obedience of Jesus; we call it The Bible; of course, to the Jews and back then The Bible was only 5 books (The Talmud). The Bible is a library of 66 books all telling a love story and giving illustrations of people promoting God's love to the Jewish people, and then beyond the Jewish people to the world (The Catholics use a Bible with between 73 and 82 books).

Poll 2

Who would you say is a successful person?

I asked this question to the same people and, again, I received a variety of answers. Some people who had said that success meant being at peace, said that a successful person was one who could be true to him/herself and to God at the same time.

Others have said that a successful person is one who will search and research for the answers to questions and will not give up until they have the answers for which they were looking.

I have actually had people through the years tell me that to be a successful person I would need to surround myself with successful people and learn from them. But, that's a catch 22 because I wouldn't know who was a successful person, so that I could hang around him (her). It's like getting a good job. A college degree doesn't help if you haven't been working for anyone doing what you are applying for.

Here is a quote from one man that I polled, "Successful people are those that never surrender themselves to settle. They set goals, accomplish them, then set new goals for themselves to reach. They always want to be a better person then they were when they woke up this morning."

Some said that a successful person is one who can find the good in whatever happens in life. People try their best to do a good job where they are, at Wal-mart, Sears, Target, Dillard's, K-mart or Macy's, or one of the millions of other jobs that they might have, so that they can be happy and content with their place of employment. To them that is being a successful person.

My friend Simon Barrett, a reporter and book reviewer said, "Twenty years ago I would have found this question easy to answer. People making huge sums of money. Today, I am not so sure that I buy into that story. The people I admire and view as successful, are not rich, and you would never hear about them on the TV. Mostly they are unknown names, yet they have overcome obstacles to follow a dream. Some have overcome health problems; some have battled just to get out of poverty and homelessness. Some have learned to read and write. These are the people that I view as successful."

He has a good point. A while ago I might have said that successful people were the rich in the monetary arena also because, as it seemed, everyone looked to them for help. But those people were more like Ebenezer Scrooge than anyone who would spread the wealth. They might not be like Scrooge in the flaunting it area; Scrooge did not flaunt the fact that he had money.

Barbra Smith, a secretary at Victory Christian Center said this about successful people, "Successful person? Living examples are: Billy Graham, T.L. Osborn, Nelson Mandela, George Bush(s), Joyce Meyer—people who's life of service has impacted individuals and nations. Examples now in Heaven include leaders like Ronald Reagan, Winston Churchill, Oral Roberts, Kenneth Hagin, and our precious Pastor Billy Joe Daugherty—people who never pulled back from their assignment, ran their race strong, and left a legacy in generations of lives they touched." Some of these people I don't know but all of them have or had a goal set for them by God. They saw what they had to do and they did it, and didn't let adversity hold them back.

These people were leaders and people who were in the limelight. But what Simon Barrett had said about successful people being those who are relatively unknown is also true. I, personally, know of some successful people who will never be known outside of their small community.

Steve Carney, fellow author and teacher, says this about successful people, "A successful person is one who hears God and does His will; one who is a friend of God." Being a friend of God does not simply mean confessing Jesus as Lord. The patriarch Abraham was a friend of God.

Now, here is my personal definition of a successful person; a person who is led by God, loves, honors and obeys Jesus and makes a difference. Whether the person accomplishes anything that would impress anyone is purely irrelevant, as long as that person is doing what he is doing by God's grace.

There is one great emotion that will come against everyone that wants to be successful in life, and that is FEAR, not the fear of the Lord. A good acronym for FEAR is False

Evidence Appearing Real. The truly successful person will or has had opportunities to be overcome by fear and has, in the past, overcome it. But, he or she will have that opportunity again and again. Fear is a relentless foe; actually fear is a tool of the devil, the enemy to all success. And since fear comes at you all the time, you have the opportunity to overcome it more than once. A good verse to remember for each time the devil tries to throw fear at you is,

> "God did not give us a spirit that makes us afraid but a spirit of power and love and self-control," (2 Timothy 1:7 New Century Version).

If God did not give you a spirit of fear then why would you be hanging around with it?

Chapter 3

Moses

Moses was a man who was born in slavery; his parents were slaves in Egypt. Fact is, if not for the grace of God and the love and will of his parents, Moses would have been killed at birth. The edict of Pharaoh was,

> "When you are helping the Hebrew women during childbirth on the delivery stool, if you see that the baby is a boy, kill him; but if it is a girl, let her live," (Exodus 1:16 New International Version).

But Moses' real mother hid him for three months, the Hebrew midwife must have helped, and then made a waterproofed basket—

an ark—and floated him on the Nile. Pharaoh's daughter found him and raised him as her own; an Israelite slave raised as an Egyptian free man.

Later, Moses killed an Egyptian and was exiled to wonder in the desert. He happened upon the Midianites who lived in the desert.

> "Pharaoh heard about it and tried to kill Moses, but Moses got away to the land of Midian. He sat down by a well," (Exodus 2:15 The Message).

Soon, Moses saw a very intriguing vision in the desert, it was a bush that was burning but was not consumed.

> "And the Angel of the LORD appeared to him in a flame of fire from the midst of a bush. So he looked, and behold, the bush was burning with fire, but the bush *was* not consumed," (Exodus 3:2 New King James Version).

Was Moses successful at this point? Remember, he was a prince in one of the most powerful nations in the world at the time. But, although he was touching many lives, he didn't even know whom the true and living God was (being before Jesus came to Earth he wouldn't have been able to obey Jesus). So, no, he wasn't truly successful.

34

But when he walked up to the bush he met God. To make a long story short, God gave Moses instructions about what He wanted him to do. Like most men and women today, Moses began with the excuses for why he couldn't do what God told him. But, one by one, God dissolved each excuse. Finally, God gave Aaron as Moses' mouthpiece because Moses insisted that he couldn't speak properly.

> "Then the LORD's anger burned against Moses and he said, "What about your brother, Aaron the Levite? I know he can speak well. He is already on his way to meet you, and he will be glad to see you," (Exodus 4:14 New International Version).

Although God's anger was kindled He was still merciful. He could have sent Aaron and said, "Nix you, Moses." Instead, He added Aaron to the ministry that Moses was to carry out. So, the lesson we all can learn from this is don't make excuses and anger God because He can take your ministry and give it to someone else.

So, was Moses successful now? He had just gotten instructions from the living God. No, he wasn't yet and if he kept his excuses alive he wouldn't be, period. He hadn't yet done anything that God had told him; he hadn't touched one life since he met God. He hadn't even started back toward Egypt yet; he just met God. No obedience.

But then, as he made up his mind to do what the Lord had told him to do he entered the realm of a successful man; he started back towards Egypt. Now, according to that one man who said, "For me success is when one sets themselves towards honorable goals and endlessly strives to meet said goals," Moses was successful right then. He had set an honorable goal—set by the Lord, actually. But, he was only starting out, wasn't he. So, the successful part might be thought of as a little pre-mature because Moses hadn't touched one life yet; or had he? What about Aaron's life? Did Moses affect his life?

Most of you know the story about what happened after Moses had returned to Egypt so I won't reiterate that; you can go back and read the book of Exodus later. But while the children of Israel and the others were following Moses in the wilderness—Saudi Arabia—Moses had to defend the children before God. He had to put up with plenty of grief from the children, who are a good representation of baby Christians; but

Moses was gracious enough to be move by God to meet their needs.

> "And Moses stretched out his hand over the sea; and when the morning appeared, the sea returned to its full depth, while the Egyptians were fleeing into it. So the LORD overthrew the Egyptians in the midst of the sea. Then the waters returned and covered the chariots, the horsemen, *and* all the army of Pharaoh that came into the sea after them. Not so much as one of them remained. But the children of Israel had walked on dry *land* in the midst of the sea, and the waters *were* a wall to them on their right hand and on their left."
>
> "So the LORD saved Israel that day out of the hand of the Egyptians, and Israel saw the Egyptians dead on the seashore. Thus Israel saw the great work which the LORD had done in Egypt; so the people feared the LORD, and believed the LORD and His servant Moses," (Exodus 14:27-31 New King James Version).

This is only the first of many miracles done through the hands of Moses after they left the borders of Egypt.

There was a time when Moses got ripping mad. The children were grumbling about having no water. This is what the Lord said to Moses and Aaron,

> "Take the staff, and you and your brother Aaron gather the assembly together. Speak to that rock before their eyes and it will pour out its water. You will bring water out of the rock for the community so they and their livestock can drink," (Numbers 20:8 New International Version).

But this is what Moses did,

> "Then Moses raised his arm and **struck** the rock **twice** with his staff. Water gushed out, and the community and their livestock drank," (Numbers 20:11 New International Version).

Who is the rock of our salvation? Jesus, right. In John 19:34 the Roman soldier stuck Jesus in His side. But the reason why I said that Moses was angry is because he struck it twice, not just once; also the fact that God told him to speak to the rock and he struck the rock. And because of this God told Moses that he would not go into the land promised to Israel.

Elijah

Elijah was a prophet of God during the time of King Ahab. One day he announced to Ahab that there was coming a drought, with no definite end.

> "And then this happened: Elijah the Tishbite, from among the settlers of Gilead, confronted Ahab: "As surely as GOD lives, the God of Israel before whom I stand in obedient service, the next years are going to see a total drought—not a drop of dew or rain unless I say otherwise," (1 Kings 17:1 The Message).

Why did Elijah say, "unless I say otherwise"? I believe that he said that because he knew of no other prophets of God in Israel; either that or God had already told him that his word would be the changing point. In three years (1 kings 18:2) that point of change came about.

Okay, because he did this Elijah too suffered. There came a point where he had no more food nor water. He was told by God to go down to the brook across the Kerith Ravine.

> "So he did what the LORD had told him. He went to the Kerith

Ravine, east of the Jordan, and stayed there. The ravens brought him bread and meat in the morning and bread and meat in the evening, and he drank from the brook," (1 Kings 17:5-6 New International Version).

When the brook dried up Elijah was sent somewhere else. The Lord told Elijah,

"Arise, go to Zarephath, which *belongs* to Sidon, and dwell there. See, I have commanded a widow there to provide for you," (1 King 17:9 King James Version).

Even though the Lord had commanded her, she didn't listen. Some may read this next verse and think that Elijah had missed God; but the woman wasn't walking with God so even though God did speak to her (He speaks to everyone whether they listen or not) she wasn't tuned in.

"As she was going to get it, he called, 'And bring me, please, a piece of bread.'

"'As surely as the LORD your God lives,' she replied, 'I don't have any bread—only a handful of flour in a jar and a little olive oil in a jug. I am gathering a few sticks to take home and make a meal for myself and my son, that we may eat it—and die.'"

(1 Kings 11-12 New International
Version).

Was Elijah confused? Did he pick the
wrong woman? No, but sometimes we (you and
I) have to go by what the Lord told us about the
situation even against what things look like or
what other people say. Notice she said, "As
surely as the LORD *your* God lives." Now,
what does that tell you? He wasn't her God.

So anyway, Elijah told her what the
Lord said and she *accepted it* and did
accordingly; and God's Word worked.

A while later Elijah visits another
woman and her husband. They would represent,
what I call, nominal Christians; they believed in
God but lived in sin ("After all, we are just
sinners saved by grace," although that's not true
at all). They even built a room for this man of
God. And God, through Elijah decided to do
something special for them so He gave her a
son.

Soon the son dies and she goes to the
prophet to berate him.

> "The woman said to Elijah,
> 'Why did you ever show up here in the
> first place—a holy man barging in,

exposing my sins, and killing my son?'" (1 Kings 17:18 The Message).

But, what did Elijah do? He didn't let that berating get to him; it would have categorically stopped him. This happens to many people trying to do the will of God, they get berated because the devil interrupted and the blame falls to the man of God, and this stops many men because they just can't take it. This doesn't mean the man of God simply falls away from claiming to believe, he just doesn't do anything about it.

The son was brought back to life because Elijah wouldn't quit. Read 1 Kings 17:24, you will see what the woman said when Elijah gave her the boy, alive. I find it interesting that she didn't say, "I'm sorry I doubted you," or something to the effect of an apology. You might do an act of God for someone and never even get an acknowledgement of the deed done; don't let that stop you.

King Ahab and his wife Jezebel were evil, they served the devil, they hated Elijah with a passion because Elijah represented their enemy, God. Now, Elijah worked many wonders of God in the presence of all Israel. He even challenged the prophets of Baal to a sacrifice duel. They had no results and, now, this is interesting. Allow me to quote.

> "And he put the wood in order, cut the bull in pieces, and laid *it* on the wood, and said, 'Fill four waterpots with water, and pour *it* on the burnt sacrifice and on the wood.' Then he said, 'Do *it* a second time,' and they did *it* a second time; and he said, 'Do *it* a third time,' and they did *it* a third time. So the water ran all around the altar; and he also filled the trench with water." (1 King 18:33-35 New King James Version).

This may make it look like Elijah got prideful, but he was only doing this as the Lord was telling him. He was proud of the Lord's wondrous abilities to show up these 'nothing' worshippers, but not proud of himself; after all, he saw himself as only a poor servant. Where do you stand?

So, then Elijah prayed and fire came out of heaven, and God had a good meal plus water to make it go down easier.

Then Elijah got word that Jezebel wanted to kill him so he ran into the wilderness. Elijah wasn't popular, especially with the king and queen, and when you make up your mind that you are going to do God's will no matter what, you will not be popular to too many either. But God will treasure you above many.

Chapter 4

Uzziah

Uzziah, son of Amaziah—king of Judah, was a good, godly man. The people made him king when he was just sixteen years old. He reigned for 52 years.

The man sought God daily and learned plenty. He did good as king and he became famous, he fought the Philistines and defeated them and many of their fortified cities. Other nations paid tribute to King Uzziah and the Lord was with him.

He contracted for watchtowers to be built at the gates of Jerusalem for protection (2 Chronicles 26:9). He amassed a great army for both offence and defense, and he amassed sheep and cattle. Farmers were under his employ because he loved growing things.

This reminds us of the Christian life in that we are called to build up the Christian way of life with the truth of God's Word, pray and build 'a hedge of protection' around our fellows, and grow disciples. King Uzziah would have been thought of as the perfect representation of a successful man, until self-pride weaseled in.

Because he was king and he had all these successes; he was very rich, his army was feared, he was very popular, he had plenty of farmers working for him, all that good stuff; he became puffed up.

> "Now about food sacrificed to idols: We know that 'We all possess knowledge.' But knowledge puffs up while love builds up," (1 Corinthians 8:1 New International Version).

One thing about love, it's got to be operated in all the time. It's one thing to have love—if you have Jesus, you have love; Paul had love—but it's entirely another to operate in love. Look at 1 Corinthians 13:1-3, you can't do those things if you don't *have* love. But, you can have love and not operate in love.

So, the knowledge of what Uzziah did got him caught up in self-pride and he did something that was a major violation of God's Law, his own law, and The Temple Law.

> "But then the strength and success went to his head. Arrogant and proud, he fell. One day, contemptuous of GOD, he walked into The Temple of GOD like he owned it and took over, burning incense on the Incense Altar. The priest Azariah, backed up by eighty brave priests of GOD, tried to prevent him. They confronted Uzziah: 'You must not, you *cannot* do this, Uzziah—only the Aaronite priests, especially consecrated for the work, are permitted to burn incense. Get out of God's Temple; you are unfaithful and a disgrace!'" (2 Chronicles 26:16-18 The Message).

You will notice that it wasn't even every priest who could burn incense, but only the ones 'consecrated for the work,' (Look back at Exodus and read about Aaron and The Temple).

David

The most famous king in the Old Testament is King David, and one of the reasons he is so famous is because he became a royal failure who did something so amazing that God loves him so much. "What did he do?" you might ask. He repented.

Let's look, first, at David's humble beginnings; well not all the way back. When David made his first appearance in the Bible he was a shepherd (the Bible doesn't say anything about age but he was a boy). The one distinctive factor that would separate him from other boys of his time is that he loved his Lord immensely.

Samuel, *the* prophet during King Saul's reign, was told by the Lord to go to the house of Jesse, David's dad. He was there to anoint a new king over Israel because God did not approve of Saul anymore. David was the youngest and the runt of a family with eight sons; but David was the one that Samuel was to anoint.

Soon after that King Saul had a need for him at the palace to play music for him. Actually, he frequently visited the palace for that very reason, although nothing more is written about David for a time.

When Israel and the Philistines decided to take up and have a war David's brothers went to fight for Saul, but David was to young to go. Jesse sent David to bring supplies to his brothers and while he was there he heard a Philistine giant berating the God of Israel. When David heard this—this dummy smelling up the place—he got mad.

> "Then David spoke to the men who stood by him, saying, 'What shall be done for the man who kills this Philistine and takes away the reproach from Israel? For who *is* this uncircumcised Philistine, that he should defy the armies of the living God?'" (1 Samuel 17:26 New King James Version).

Anyone standing around could just tell that David was hot. This fool, Goliath, was talking about his God, and not in a nice way either. So, David got the king's permission and he went down and vented his anger on the Philistine giant.

When David killed the Philistine 'joke' he rapidly grew in popularity; David didn't do this to become popular, it just happened that way. He was content where he was, '*Let Saul keep the thrown, I just want to serve my God,*' is what David thought.

David became best buds with Saul's son, Jonathon, who loved David as himself. When Saul went crazy-to-the-max he threw a spear at Jonathon because Jonathon had let David go into hiding. So, now David is popular with some but on the wanted list with the king, and I don't mean dead or alive.

Much later David was king, and in that time Kings went to war every year—for some reason. But one time King David decided to stay at home in His palatial palace. One evening he was up on his balcony and he happened to look out over the houses. Women use to bath out on their roofs in the fresh rainwater. David had a loyal warrior named Uriah, he had one wife named Bathsheba whom David saw taking a bath on her roof. He took a second look and a third look, '*I like,*' he thought. (This is why I said He became a royal failure). He sent for her and things led to more things, and sexual sin was produced. As if that wasn't bad enough, she found that she was pregnant; so David wound up killing Uriah.

Now, Nathan, the Prophet for David of that time, came to David and told him what he did, and David pronounced judgment. Then Nathan told David that he was the one who did the brutal act. David repented (Psalm 51). But the sin still had its effects. That should tell you that you can't go around sinning and repenting and think that just because you repented then there will be no effects of your sin.

David had sons and a daughter by more than one wife (well, that was custom at the time in Israel). One son lusted after his daughter and another son killed him. This is an effect of that sin, there would be turmoil in the family.

Some of you may think that David rose to a successful position when he became king, but then he became a jerk when he took Bathsheba, and he never really got back to his position of success because of the turmoil in the family. But, no, David began to be successful when he was back in that field tending those sheep and singing to God. He never really lost his position of being successful; he just changed social positions and spiritual status (he rose to be king, he sinned and he repented).

King David died a successful man with plenty of admirers, he had gold, silver, all kinds of livestock, you name it, chances are he had it. But that's not what David based his success on and that's not what made him a successful man.

According to 1 Samuel 13:14 David was a man after God's own heart. That, my friend, is the key to David's success. Saul had lost his right to be called a successful person when he decided that he knew better than God. And you cannot have even an inkling of success without being, like David, a man or woman after God's own heart. But that's not all that attributed to David's success. He did what God told him to do; he stood up against the behemoth Goliath, he led the armies of Israel to multiple victories, and when he sinned he repented.

Chapter 5

Jeremiah

Jeremiah was a priest and a prophet in Judah during the time when 10 tribes of Israel broke off from the remaining 2 tribes; they were called (the northern tribes) Israel; and (the southern tribes—Judah and Benjamin) were called Judah.   King Josiah of Judah was a righteous man and he was a friend to Jeremiah, but after Josiah was killed his son took kingship; and the son wasn't good at all.   Half way through Josiah's reign Jeremiah accepted his calling into the prophetic ministry.

As a prophet, Jeremiah was very obedient to his God, Yahweh, and as a result he had some pretty harsh things to say, and He made many serious enemies.

At one point Jeremiah was beat and thrown into a cage where he was put on public display, much like a betrayed beast. I guess the wicked king figured, "Let's make an example of him, telling Jerusalem that anyone who speaks against the (evil) acts of us (wicked people) will be so treated."

Jeremiah sure had plenty of reason to feel down-in-the-mouth (thought he did) but the Lord reaffirmed him.

At the time of Jeremiah's prophetic ministry there was little to no support for him; the righteous king was dead and the priesthood was not 100% for Yahweh either.

But Jeremiah was no ordinary prophet; some of his prophecies were not only for Judah and Israel in that era, but for the Church in America today. You wouldn't think that that would be possible, but while I was reading Jeremiah 3:6-11 I realized that he was talking about here and now. Then, verses 15-16 of chapter 3 talk about pastors; spiritual shepherds are pastors.

Jonah

Jonah was a prophet, a very righteous man. He enjoyed the favor and blessings of God.

The book of Jonah is not very descript, it is too short and does not tell the whole story. So, I asked the Lord to tell me why Jonah didn't want to go to Nineveh. Nineveh was located north of Babylon on the Tigris River. Needless to say it was not an Israeli city, and their god was not Yahweh. These people had attacked Israel before; and, although Jonah had never met a Ninevite, he had heard some very horrible stories about them. Besides all that, they did not have a covenant with the almighty God.

So, when God told Jonah to go to Nineveh and speak over it, Jonah thought, '*Wait a dog gone minute*,' and he took off in the opposite direction. Jonah reasoned with himself that since Nineveh was such a rotten tomato, as the stories said, and they had no covenant with God, what would God (Yahweh) have to do with them. He reasoned that either he heard a strangers voice (John 10:5) or God must have been wrong. But deep down Jonah knew it was

Yahweh about Nineveh and this was something that God wanted him to do.

So Jonah ran, was thrown off a ship and almost drown, but God still loved Jonah and appointed a fish to give him a sub-marine ride. Jonah was on the verge of failure, but the fish intervened; that is where Jonah made the important change, he repented, and decided to honor God's wishes.

So God gives the fish a bellyache and Jonah comes out of the fish accompanied by...sludge. But Jonah was now starting his life of being a success again and now he had made the quality decision and set his face (2 Kings 12:17) to go to Nineveh.

To Jonah's surprise, Nineveh was more God-fearing than he thought; they repented at Jonah's word, but Jonah still wanted to see them burn. Jonah had a little more growing to do. While Jonah was sitting on a hill in the desert waiting for God to strike Nineveh God had a plant to grow up, rather rapidly, to give him some shade. But over night God sent a caterpillar to eat the plant and make it fail. Jonah didn't like that but God said to him,

> "But the LORD said, 'You have been concerned about this plant,

> though you did not tend it or make it
> grow. It sprang up overnight and died
> overnight. And should I not have
> concern for the great city of Nineveh,
> in which there are more than a hundred
> and twenty thousand people who
> cannot tell their right hand from their
> left—and also many animals?'" (Jonah
> 4:10-11 New International Version).

After all, God reasoned that they too are seed of Noah who was His creation, which makes all mankind God's creation, whether they are good or bad.

Jesus

Israel had been seeking the Messiah (the anointed deliverer) for an abundance of years. The timing was ripe and God turned to Himself and said it is time. Then Gabriel, the announcer angle, went to the town of Nazareth, to a young girl named Mary and said,

> "'Don't be afraid, Mary,' the
> angel told her, 'for you have found
> favor with God! You will conceive and
> give birth to a son, and you will name
> him Jesus. He will be very great and

> will be called the Son of the Most
> High. The Lord God will give him the
> throne of his ancestor David. And he
> will reign over Israel forever; his
> Kingdom will never end!'" (Luke 1:30-
> 33 New Living Translation).

Jesus was born; a baby came into this world through the womb of a virgin.

> "'How will this be,' Mary
> asked the angel, 'since I am a
> virgin?'" (Luke 1:34 New
> International Version).

Jesus came to the Earth as a man; and how was he received? Well, some shepherd were told by angels (the angels were having a hilarious time) of the glorious arrival, and astronomers (magi) from the orient knew of a great birth, but nothing else. In fact even thought John, the baptizer, had been preparing the way not many of the religious folk even cared to investigate, not until Jesus began His earthly ministry.

> "But made himself of no
> reputation, and took upon him the form
> of a servant, and was made in the
> likeness of men: And being found in
> fashion as a man, he humbled himself,
> and became obedient unto death, even
> the death of the cross," (Philippians
> 2:7-8 King James Version).

Don't get me wrong, it was a glorious occasion. But seriously, to most of the Jews, especially most of the religious Jews, the birth of Jesus meant very little if anything.

Although Jesus was God's Word made flesh, 100% God, He was also 100% man and He lived on Earth and carried Himself as a man, without all the godly attributes.

> "Do you think I cannot call on my Father, and he will at once put at my disposal more than twelve legions of angels? But how then would the Scriptures be fulfilled that say it must happen in this way?" (Matthew 26:54 New International Version).

Jesus did very many miracles while He was on the Earth *in one physical body*. And it is a foregone conclusive fact that Jesus was the epitome of success when He was on Earth as one man. But Luke, the one who wrote the book of Acts, said that Jesus only began His ministry.

> "IN THE former account [which I prepared], O Theophilus, I made [a continuous report] dealing with all the things which Jesus began to do and to teach," (Acts 1:1 Amplified Bible).

You must know that Jesus rose from the dead; and if He began something it would only make sense that He would be continuing that very something. This is where the Church comes into the picture. Through you and me He wants to continue His actions of success.

Chapter 6

Mary

When the angel of God came to Mary and announced that she, a virgin, would get pregnant without a man she could have blown the whole deal.

For a woman who never married, to be pregnant was totally forbidden and a crime worthy of stoning to death in ancient Israel; well for us in 21-century America it is not right either. It meant that she was playing the harlot and although harlotry was and is practiced it was and is looked down upon by the majority.

> "The angel answered her, 'The Holy Spirit will come to you, and the power of the Most High will

overshadow you. Therefore, the holy child developing inside you will be called the Son of God,'" (Luke 1:35 GOD'S WORD).

As it seemed at the time, harlotry was what Gabriel was asking Mary to do; but that wasn't true. God knew His Law and He wasn't about to break His Law, or the laws set down by the council of elders for that matter. So, what God was really asking her—and this is purely my thoughts on the matter—was "Mary, will you marry Me and have My baby?" Of coarse, this was a spiritual marriage; it had nothing to do with Joseph.

There is not much written about the life of Mary after the birth of Jesus but we do know that she held onto the faith that He was the One who people all around claimed that He was/is, our Lord and Savior. She was not a rich woman, in monetary goods, but she was well taken care of because she was Mary, the mother of our Lord.

Peter

Before his name was changed to Peter it was Simon. Now, Simon was a fisherman until Jesus came into his life and said those famous words, "Follow Me."

> "Then He said to them, 'Follow Me, and I will make you fishers of men,'" (Matt. 4:19 New King James Version).

Jesus put out the bait that Simon needed to hear and Simon, being no fool, took the bait and followed Jesus. But that wasn't the beginning of his success; it did not start yet.

By reading the four synoptic gospels you can deduce that Simon was a loud mouth, a 'do it my way' type of guy, a leaf blown in the wind.

Many people seem to think that Jesus change Simon's name to Peter because he had the revelation that Jesus is the Son of God; but if that were so then everyone who has had that revelation would be named Peter. Peter does mean rock but the rock that Jesus built his Church on is the rock of revelation that Peter had.

Now, why was Simon renamed Peter? Another meaning of Peter is steady or firm, not vacillating to and fro. Although this is not the meaning of the name Simon, Simon was a wavering leaf; Jesus renamed him Peter as a goal to become a steady rock. Just because Jesus renamed him Peter at the time he made the confession doesn't mean that he was already a steady rock. If he was then why would Peter have done those things that he did, rebuking the Master and impetuously cutting off the ear of the high priests' servant?

When he made that faith filled confession that Jesus is the Lord (the Son of God) was the point of beginning of Peter's success. But Peter had a long way to go before he really could be called a successful person.

On one of the days that Jesus was talking about when He said,

> "At that time you won't need to ask me for anything. I tell you the truth, you will ask the Father directly, and he will grant your request because you use my name," (John 16:23 New Living Translation),

Peter prayed, but he did not pray in the name of Jesus; and he cast lots to find the answer to their prayer.

> "And they proposed two: Joseph called Barsabas, who was surnamed Justus, and Matthias. And they prayed and said, 'You, O Lord, who know the hearts of all, show which of these two You have chosen to take part in this ministry and apostleship from which Judas by transgression fell, that he might go to his own place.' And they cast their lots, and the lot fell on Matthias. And he was numbered with the eleven apostles," (Acts 1:23-26 New King James Version).

This was not a prayer in the name of Jesus, that Jesus said would work (John 16:23), and it wasn't God's will to have Matthias in Judas's spot; if you will read further in Acts you will see that it was Paul. God wasn't using the lot system anymore; He was using the system of prayer in Jesus' name. And Peter soon realized that, as did the rest of the disciples.

Soon, Peter began living as a successful man because after he had received the baptism in the Holy Spirit (God) he began letting God use him to do His will. God had a vision for Peter and He shared it with him.

> "Where there is no vision, the people perish: but he that keepeth the law, happy is he," (Proverbs 29:18 King James Version).

The successfulness of Peter came into fruition when he was doing God's will in accordance with the particular vision that God had given him.

Judas

> "David went out to meet them and said to them, 'If you have come to me in peace to help me, I am ready for you to join me. But if you have come to betray me to my enemies when my hands are free from violence, may the God of our ancestors see it and judge you,'" (1 Chronicles 12:17 New International Version).

As you know, Judas was a thief before he started following Jesus. He was probably a thief for a while even after he started following Jesus and listening to His teaching.

Now, this is my conjecture, if you don't want to believe it that's your decision, it won't keep you from heaven. But, I believe that the teachings of the Master had sunken into the man's heart and Judas no longer wanted to be a thief. He probably went to Jesus for help putting down the thief's life-style. But everywhere the company went there were things that worked to draw Judas back to the thieving style in which he was use to living. At times Judas seemed to be doing okay; but then there were times like when Jesus was anointed at the house of Lazarus.

> 'So they made Him a supper; and Martha served, but Lazarus was one of those at the table with Him. Mary took a pound of ointment of pure liquid nard [a rare perfume] that was very expensive, and she poured it on Jesus' feet and wiped them with her hair. And the whole house was filled with the fragrance of the perfume. But Judas Iscariot, the one of His disciples who was about to betray Him, said, 'Why was this perfume not sold for 300 denarii [a year's wages for an ordinary workman] and that [money] given to the poor (the destitute)?''' (John 12:2-5 Amplified Bible).

Now, the next verse says that he said what he said because he was a thief and not because he cared for the poor. Well, he was a thief, although trying to get out of that way of thought. Just like a recovering alcoholic always has alcoholic thoughts in the back of his mind, so Judas, as a recovering thief, had thieving in the back of his mind.

Even though he probably went to Jesus for help he may not have followed through with the help that he got. With people that go to a doctor to get help to quit something the doctor gives them a program to follow. Many of those people fall back into their old way of life: why? Because they are too lazy to do what they need to do, either that or they don't really want to change. Just so, Judas went to Jesus for help and Jesus 'put him on a program.' Either Judas was too lazy to keep up with the program or he didn't really want to change.

The devil knew whom he/it could use to betray Jesus so he/it entered the scene and took control of Judas and tempted him with thirty pieces of silver (price for a slave). Knowing that the Pharisees did not like Jesus, Judas went to them,

> "and said, "What are you willing to give me if I deliver Him to you?" And they counted out to him thirty pieces of silver," (Matthew 26:15 New King James Version).

Now, whether Judas knew they were going to kill Jesus or not, I don't really know, because after Jesus was crucified Judas went back to those same Pharisees and cried,

> "'I have sinned,' he said, 'for I have betrayed innocent blood.'
>
> "'What is that to us?' they replied. 'That's your responsibility.' So Judas threw the money into the temple and left. Then he went away and hanged himself," (Matthew 27:4-5 New International Version).

One version of verse 3, the verse just before these verses, says that Judas repented. Because of that one verse some people think that Judas might be in heaven. But Jesus said earlier that,

> "While I was with them in the world, I kept them in thy name: those that thou gavest me I have kept, and none of them is lost, but the son of perdition; that the scripture might be fulfilled," (John 17:12 King James Version).

Judas, I believe, tried, but he was not a success because he set aside the truth of God's Word for money and,

> "No one can serve two masters. Either you will hate the one and love the other, or you will be devoted to the one and despise the

other. You cannot serve both God and money," (Matthew 6:24 New International Version).

Chapter 7

You

What is your occupation? Do you do it with pleasing the Lord in mind or do you do it simply to make money?

When you made Jesus your Lord and decided to put Him first in your life you made a step toward the life of success. But that was only the first step in a vast journey; there are more steps.

Take an illustration: You and some of your friends decide to climb Pike's Peak. So you get your equipment and a guide and set out on your wonderful journey. You drive to a building at the base of the mountain and tell your wives to come back for you in a month. You and your friends got all psyched up and you take a step. Then you say, "Well, that was an experience that I'll never forget."

In a month you wives come back and you are camped out at the bottom of the mountain. Your wife asks you, "What did you do about the surprise hurricane that occurred up there ten days ago?"

Not willing to lie to your wife you say, "What hurricane?"

Ok, I know, you're thinking, *'That's stupid. I wouldn't climb Pike's Peak. Besides, if I did decide to climb it I would not take one step and lie about the experience.'* Well, that's what you're doing when you accept Jesus and don't continue doing what He said to do.

Take another illustration: You are going water-skiing. So, you get your skies, the boat and sit out on the dock, all prepared for your day; or so you think. Do you have your life vest? Ok, so you have the proper equipment; do you know how to water-ski? Ok, so you know how to water-ski and you are totally prepared. Ok, now you sit on the dock all set to go and the boat is starting up. The boat pulls you along but you are having troubles because of the wake of the motor. You try to jump the waves but you fall on your face and lose hold of the rope. Are you sure that you knew how to water-ski? In the class they would have instructed you in what to do about the motor wake. Maybe you should go back and pay attention when they talk about that subject.

It seems like you—whoever the you that was water-skiing is—tried to go from thinking about water-skiing to jumping in the water.

When you were born did you graduate from graduate school with a master's degree? I didn't think so. No, that would be ridiculous to even think that. Well, in the same way, when you are born again (born of God) you have to grow and learn. No one who is just born again (as in one second old) is ready to rule beside Jesus, or pastor a church or teach in a seminary, or whatever. In other words, when you are just born again you have taken the first step. Now you have to grow and learn to achieve success.

The Holy Spirit And You

"And you know that God anointed Jesus of Nazareth with the Holy Spirit and with power. Then Jesus went around doing good and healing all who were oppressed by the devil, for God was with him," (Acts 10:38 New Living Translation).

There is not one version or translation of the Holy Bible where that verse says that God anointed Jesus *Christ*. Can you guess why that is? That is simply because Christ means the anointed one.

You say that you want to be like Jesus; well Jesus received the baptism in the Holy Spirit. He was water baptized, he was Holy Spirit baptized, He laid hands on the sick and they recovered, he spoke in tongues (John 11:33). And then He said,

"Very truly I tell you, whoever believes in me will do the works I have been doing, and they will do even greater things than these, because I am going to the Father," (John 14:12 New International Version).

Success comes when you are doing God's Word. Christians want to be disciples of Jesus and, eventually, to go to heaven; this would mean they are successful.

> "Then Jesus turned to the Jews who had claimed to believe in him. 'If you stick with this, living out what I tell you, you are my disciples for sure. Then you will experience for yourselves the truth, and the truth will free you,'" (John 8:31-32 The Message)

If you claim to believe then put your name in place of those Jews who had claimed to believe because Jesus *is* talking to you.

The Lord knows what you can do and what you cannot do. But He is not looking for what you can do in the natural; He is looking for your availability to be used by Him. Paul said,

> "I can do all things through Christ who strengthens me," (Philippians 4:13 New King James Version).

God might want to use you right where you are, that would make you successful if you gave yourself to Him. Or He might want to use you in something else; He may want you to quite your job and follow Him, just like He did with

Simon Bar Jonah and Matthew; that would also make for a successful life.

In the past there have been many people who were in the flow of success, but then stepped out of the way of success and totally lost everything. They got confused or mislead or they let self-pride or wrongful events get to them and they fell away.

"What do you mean by self-pride? I thought pride was pride," you might say. These people started out doing God's Will and they were blessed beyond what many of you could imagine. But because they saw that they were getting so popular they began to get conceited and started being picky about what they would do and whom they would do it for. They wound up leaving God behind because they got it in their head that they put themselves in that high position.

You want to start your successful journey with Jesus and the Holy Spirit. And you definitely want to, indeed, need to stay with Him and obey His Word. But you want to carry it out to the end because, as a friend said, if you are 99.99% obedient and .01% undisciplined then that .01% could, very well, be your downfall.

A Package Deal

Earlier, I wrote an article where Jesus asked, "Do You Love Me?" In that article we saw the marriage phrase, "Do you... promise to love, honor and obey...?" Those three words are actually viewed as one word when Jesus asked you if you love Him, truly love Him.

With many couples when they get married and the reverend says, "Do you... promise to love, honor and obey..." they have a disability (for lack of a better word) called 'selective hearing.' What they heard was probably something like this, "Do you love...?" And they also have a limited definition of love.

They, selectively, missed, at least, three words; the first word that they might/probably have missed is very, very important. That word is **promise**. A promise is something that God does not take lightly at all, in other words a promise is *not* to be broken, it's a do or die matter with God. The second and third words are part of love and explain a little more what love does; yes, does. Love is an action word (the dictionary may call love strictly a noun, but Jesus equates it to doing),

"Jesus said to his disciples: If you love me, you will do as I command," (John 14:15 Contemporary English Version).

"Do you love Me?" This is the question that Jesus is asking you. He asked the same question of Peter in the book of John; He asked it three times and He emphasized loving Himself over the others.

"If people come to me and are not ready to abandon their fathers, mothers, wives, children, brothers, and sisters, as well as their own lives, they cannot be my disciples," (Luke 14:26 GOD'S WORD).

Many people, people who want to be thought of as real Christians, will give an instant yes to Jesus' question. But their love is more selective than anyone knows.

What if God were to tell them to do something like, "in the middle of your sermon stop, take a coin from your pocket and place it on your arm. Then take that coin and flip it in the air, catch it and look at it. Then put it back in your pocket and continue your sermon."? What if He told you to do something so ridiculous as that? Some of those 'real Christians' would think, 'what will people think *of me? I'll look like a fool.'* They simply wouldn't do it. Would you do what God told you even if it made you look like a fool?

In the book of Acts chapter 8, Philip was in a Samaritan town preaching to gospel. There was a man there named Simon who practiced magic arts, he enjoyed being thought of as someone great. When Philip preached everyone turned to Jesus; even Simon turned, or so he wanted everyone to think. Then Peter and John went to that town because they had only received Jesus as Lord but they were not baptized in the Holy Spirit yet. Look at Acts 8:18-19,

> "Simon saw that the Spirit had been given to the believers when the apostles placed their hands on them. So he offered money to Peter and John, and said, Give this power to me too, so that anyone I place my hands on will receive the Holy Spirit," (Good News Translation).

Simon came to Jesus, but He didn't love Him more than himself. This is a pride issue disguised as love for the people. In Acts 8:22-24 we see what happens,

> "Repent of this wickedness and pray to the Lord in the hope that he may forgive you for having such a

thought in your heart. For I see that you are full of bitterness and captive to sin."

"Then Simon answered, 'Pray to the Lord for me so that nothing you have said may happen to me,'" (New International Version).

After that verse we read nothing more about Simon; I asked why. He went back to his old ways. He was still trying to grab their (the Samaritan's) attention and be thought of as someone great. You might ask, "So why didn't Peter pray for him?" Well, what did Peter tell Simon before Simon *told* him to pray for (instead of) him? God would have forgiven Simon if he repented, actually God already had forgiven him but he couldn't receive it until he repented. But Simon didn't repent; he was "full of bitterness and captive to sin."

Again, Jesus asks you, "Do you (your name) love Me?" Think about it.

One Final Note

"And don't for a minute let this Book of The Revelation be out of mind. Ponder and meditate on it day and night, making sure you practice everything written in it. Then you'll get where you're going; then you'll succeed," (Joshua 1:8 The Message).

"Never stop reciting these teachings. You must think about them night and day so that you will faithfully do everything written in them. Only then will you prosper and succeed," (Same verse GOD'S WORD).

Success begins with God and His Word; and success is your decision.

Appendix

"If you love Me, keep My commandments,"
(John 14:15 New King James Version).

"Then he breathed on them and said,
'Receive the Holy Spirit,'" (John 20:22 New
Living Translation).

"I tell you the truth, anyone who believes in
me will do the same works I have done, and
even greater works, because I am going to
be with the Father," (John 14:12 New Living
Translation).

"If you live in me and what I say lives in
you, then ask for anything you want, and it
will be yours," (John 15:7 GOD'S WORD)

"Always remember what is written in the
Book of the Teachings. Study it day and
night to be sure to obey everything that is

written there. If you do this, you will be wise and successful in everything," (Joshua 1:8 New century Version).

"I tell you for certain that if you have faith in me, you will do the same things that I am doing. You will do even greater things, now that I am going back to the Father," John 14:12 Contemporary English Version).

If you have discovered by reading this book that you need to make some changes in your life write to me and I will be more than happy to pray for you. Also, *if you would like,* I can send you some information that may help you.

Or, if you read this book and would like to know more about this ministry I would be glad to talk to you. Please write to me at the address below.

Please fill out and use the bottom of this page with your initial correspondence.

Bread of Life Int. Min.
P.O. Box 222
Little River, KS 67457
Your first name_____ Last Name_____
Mailing
Address_____
City_____State/Province_____
Country_____ Zip Code_____
Phone # where we can reach you_____
Your email
address_____

Any specific prayer requests or praise
report_____
_____
_____
_____
_____
_____
_____
_____
_____
_____(If you need to use the other side of
the page, go for it.)   It is the goal of this ministry to spread God's pure love and His Word correctly until the end comes.

Donations and gifts of Love are appreciated.